Christian Evidence Se

GW00471481

WHY
SUFFERING?

by

Sheila Cassidy
A doctor working with the terminally ill in Plymouth

Published by The Canterbury Press Norwich
for the Christian Evidence Society

First published 1993 by The Canterbury Press Norwich
(a publishing imprint of Hymns Ancient & Modern Limited, a registered charity)
St Mary's Works, St Mary's Plain,
Norwich, Norfolk, NR3 3BH

Biblical quotations are taken from the Jerusalem Bible
published by Darton Longman & Todd, 1974

British Library Cataloguing in Publication Data

A catalogue record for this book is available
from the British Library

ISBN 1-85311-078-7

Typeset by Rowland Phototypesetting Limited
Bury St Edmunds, Suffolk
Printed and bound in Great Britain by
St Edmundsbury Press Limited
Bury St Edmunds, Suffolk

Why Suffering?

WHY ME? How could God do this to me? What have I done to deserve this? It's not fair! How can you believe in a God who lets little children be hurt, abused, killed in accidents, die of cancer? Why, why? These and so many other anguished questions lie at the heart of the Christian experience, wherever men and women find themselves confronted by pain and disaster. Such questions, of course, are not new, for they are questions for all time, for all places and for all people. Ever since the first cave man wept in fury and powerlessness at the death of his wife, his friend, his child, men and women have been battering the heavens with their importunate and impossible questions. And the answer of course, never comes: or rather the questions which man works out in fury and despair when God remains silent are never really satisfactory. So, why *another* booklet on the subject, and, if I may add my own *why me*, why should I have the temerity to try and answer the ultimate questions which have defeated theologians and philosophers since time began?

Why *me*? The easy answer, of course is that I was asked to write it, and it seemed a challenge to try. The real answer, of course, is more complicated, and is caught up in the person that I am, the work that I do and my personal background. Let me explain: I am a doctor who works in a hospice for men and women with terminal cancer. This means that I am confronted on a daily basis by what is called the problem of suffering; and because I spend my life working alongside people in tragic circumstances I have been forced to listen not only to my own questions about the *why* of innocent suffering, but to those of my patients and my colleagues. This does not mean by any means that I have found the answers – simply that I have lived with these questions for many years.

Perhaps another reason that I was asked to write this booklet is that I have had an unusual personal experience of suffering. In

3

1975 while working as a doctor in South America I was detained for two months by the security forces for treating a wounded revolutionary. After my arrest I was held for three days in an interrogation centre where I was tortured with electric shocks during the course of the night. I then spent three weeks in solitary confinement and after that five weeks in a detention camp with around one hundred other women political prisoners. It was a time of great pain, loneliness and fear and has, I believe, given me some small insight into the experience of men and women who suffer powerlessness and distress of different kinds.

This then is the experiential base from which I write. Perhaps it is useful, too, to say a word about my religious background. I write as a Roman Catholic with no formal training in theology but with a certain familiarity with the scriptures built up over three years of monastic life and ten years as an occasional preacher and religious broadcaster. My interest in religion; therefore, is not so much academic as lived: my relationship with God in prayer and in mission is the cornerstone, the foundation, the anchor of my life. It is the inspiration of all that I do, the source of whatever small light I may shed.

Lastly, it is perhaps worth saying something about the manner in which I personally relate to God because it affects the way I choose to wrestle with the problem of suffering. I am one of those Christians whose experience of relationship is with the transcendent God, the unknown, mysterious God of the Old Testament, the God of Abraham, of Isaac, of Jacob and Isaiah. This means that my own way to God draws me deeper and deeper into the mystery of what has come to be known as the *Cloud of Unknowing*, that unfathomable, indescribable 'place' where the human spirit meets with the Unknown God.

Tangled threads

I have a deep sense of both the IMMANENCE, the nearness, and the TRANSCENDENCE, the otherness, of God and it is precisely this

4

experience that makes it possible for me to live peaceably with the mystery of God and his world. This is the rock upon which the small house of my faith is built, and, like a crofters cottage, it has stood fast during many violent storms. Now that you have at least some measure of your guide, let us set out together in faith to ask for ourselves the eternal WHY of suffering. We must remember, however, that this is a question which has perplexed both priests and people for thousands of years and that the answer which satisfies one person may seem either naive or incomprehensible to another. Enough. Let us begin, and because we are not theologians but ordinary people, let us take a homely image: a ball of string or wool. Perhaps if we had been the first to try to unravel this problem we might have taken firmly hold of one end and unravelled it until the other end appeared. Alas, we are not the first and we are presented with a tangled mess of threads, some of them knotted, some broken, which seem irrevocably mixed up together. Like any patient knitter, all we can do is pick a thread and gently teaze it out, seeing where it leads to.

As an Old Testament lover, I would like to take a traditional approach via the Book of Job. It is not the only entrance to the maze of the problem of suffering but it is a well trodden path and the one with which I personally am most comfortable. If you are not familiar with Job perhaps you should pause here and read it. What follows will certainly make more sense if you do, but I will try to make it intelligible anyway.

Very little is known about the writer of this book but scholars calculate that it was written about 500 years before the birth of Christ. The idea, however is much older, and is taken from an ancient pagan myth, no doubt wrestling as we are with the problem of innocent suffering. In essence, the story goes like this: Job was a GOOD man, (though not necessarily a very clever one). He was also very successful, with a large family, a flourishing business and had the respect of all who knew him. One day Satan persuades God to test Job, to see if his virtue is not really self

5

interest in disguise. God reluctantly agrees and Job not only loses all his family but develops a dreadful illness. Desolate, Job bewails his misfortune, protesting his innocence and eventually demanding that God give an account of himself. Job asks the question we all ask when disaster strikes: Why me? The central portion of the book is in the form of a dialogue between Job and four of his pious friends who try to help him come to terms with his situation. Job does not find them very helpful and eventually, in desperation, demands an answer of God. Then comes the great climax of the story, for to everyone's terror and amazement, God answers from the heart of the whirlwind. The answer, however, is not what Job or anyone else had bargained for, and that's why you and I are left 2,500 years later, still trying to untangle the knots.

A Model Christian Family

Rather than paraphrase Job's story which is written in the most wonderful poetry, I'd rather tell it in modern form, using a creation of my own, a sort of Job look-alike called Joanna. Now my Jo, of course is not a real individual, but a composite person who stands for all those who suffer through no fault of their own. If Jo's story seems a little far fetched, remember that there *are* people who suffer multiple disasters and that each misfortune that happens to her happens every single day to different individuals. For our purposes, however, poor Jo has a lot to bear.

Like Job, Joanna is a thoroughly *good* person. She is a devout Christian who obeys all the commandments, goes to church on Sundays, says her morning and night prayers, runs the Sunday School and sings in the church choir. She arranges the flowers in church, does voluntary work at the hospital, visits prisoners and unmarried mothers and is a member of Amnesty International, (not to mention Greenpeace, Friends of the Earth, the Pro-Life movement, etc.) Jo is married to Robert the man of her dreams and they have ten lovely children: Andrew, Beth, Catherine, David, Edward, Francis, George, Harry, Isobel and John. They all go to church together every Sunday and are deeply admired as a Model Christian Family.

Let's imagine this as a play: In Scene One we meet the family at Sunday lunch. Jo says grace and Robert carves the joint. Father Michael, their pastor, who has been invited to lunch, gazes around him and muses how God must love this wonderful Christian family.

In Scene Two, as in the original Job story, we move to the court of heaven where God is receiving his weekly report from the guardian angels. Rather to our surprise, Satan is there too, and God asks him what he's been up to. 'Oh, roaming about, here and there', says Satan, not wanting to let on too much about his activities. 'Have you seen my servant Joanna?', says God. 'Isn't she wonderful?. I'm so proud of her.' 'Humph!' says Satan. 'She's only good because she's scared of you. I'll bet you if things started to go wrong with her, she'd soon curse you to your face.' God is furious, but eventually agrees to let Satan test Jo, though he makes him promise not to touch a hair of her head.

Why me?

In Scene Three we move back to Jo's house. At first it seems that the house is empty and then we see a figure huddled on the sofa sobbing. It is Jo. Her shoulders heave and she rocks to and fro moaning like an animal in pain. What on earth is wrong? Then we hear the narrator's voice: the Evil one has acted swiftly and Jo's carefully ordered world has collapsed about her ears. Like a refugee, like an earthquake victim, she sits stunned and weeping amid the rubble. Then, in the sonorous tones of a wartime newscaster, the narrator reads out a list of the casualties: Robert, Jo's husband has died suddenly of a coronary. Andrew, her first born, has died in an earthquake while on voluntary service in Mexico. Beth, the first of the twins has been killed by terrorists in the Middle East while Catherine, devastated at the loss of her sister, has committed suicide. David, the ballet dancer has died of

AIDS in his London bedsit and Edward, who worked with Oxfam in Ethiopia has died of starvation in solidarity with the famine victims. Francis, the wandering poet, who cared nothing for things material, has died of an overdose of heroin in Katmandu and George, the soldier has died in battle. Harry, the student has been killed in a car crash, his sister Isobel raped and murdered, while John, the merry little boy with Downs Syndrome has died during surgery for the hole in his heart. Within a week, Jo has lost her entire family, as other women may lose those they love in time of war, famine or natural catastrophe.

The narrator's voice fades away and we, the audience, sit completely aghast. At first there is silence, a long and terrible silence, then a whisper and then a horrible keening sound, a howl of grief, like a wolf caught in a trap: 'Why, why me? What have I done to deserve this? How could God do this to me?'

The curtain falls and we file out woodenly for the intermission. Such grief is too much to handle, mind blowing to the bystander, totally devastating to those personally involved. For our purposes, let us make this intermission a long one and explore not so much the answer to the questions WHY ME? as how one approaches the questioner. The pastoral care of the afflicted (and here I mean the sick, the bereaved and all those whose lives have some how been disrupted) must be tailored not only to the man or woman and his or her situation but to the *stage* of their personal journey. The *question*, Why me? may be the same but the *response* will be different, depending upon whether it is the rhetorical wail of the recently bereft or the calculated angry question of someone struggling to make sense of his or her experience. When an individual is suddenly afflicted, finds that he or she has cancer or AIDS or multiple sclerosis, or is unexpectedly bereaved, that person frequently goes into a state of SHOCK and disbelief. It is as though the mind cuts out from the pain of reality and retreats into a world of its own. A person in such a state may *ask* 'Why me?' but is in no state to process a carefully reasoned answer. Such questions are an expression of the

8

individuals pain and need to be listened to rather than answered. More than anything, the person needs to be 'held', either metaphorically or actually, to be cocooned, and cherished until he is able to resume control of his life. This period of shock may last a few hours, days or even longer but the person will eventually emerge to experience the pain of loss.

Pangs of grief

The second stage of mourning, the phase of ACUTE GRIEF is characterized by an alternation between two states of mind: that of belief in the loss with consequent pangs of grief, pain and anger and a curious state of disbelief in which the person, unable to register the reality of his or her loss, searches for the missing person or object. Such searches, of course, are doomed to failure with a consequent sense of foolishness, frustration and renewed pain.

The emotions are very near the surface in acute grief and the bereaved experience a bewildering sequence of rage, anger, guilt and despair as they struggle to accept what is happening to them. Tears will come readily as will the 'pangs of grief', a sensation of sharp pain and despair which sweeps over people, engulfing them like a tidal wave and rendering them, for the moment, quite unable to function. Anger is a very common emotion in acute grief and it may be rational or quite irrational. It may be projected on to any available person, for example a relative or a professional carer or, in the case of a believer, it may be directed at God. It is in this situation that the question 'Why me?' may be articulated as 'How could God do this to me? How can there be a God who allows this kind of suffering. It's not fair. If God is all powerful, why doesn't he just abolish suffering?'

It is important to understand that such questions have to be *asked*, but they do not necessarily have to be *answered*. As in the earlier stage of mourning they are largely rhetorical questions, an expression of pain and grief, and much harm can be done by responding with pious platitudes when what is really needed is a listening ear and an acknowledgement of the awfulness of the situation. In most situations, the grief stricken are asking the listener to *share* their grief, not to resolve it, because they know deep down, that is not possible. This stage of grieving, then, is not really the place for offering ones carefully reasoned and lovingly cherished beliefs about the meaning of suffering. If the person actually demands to know what we think or believe it is best to speak quietly and simply to ones faith in the loving providence of God rather than enter into an explanation which may well be misunderstood or rejected. In the long run, we must all remember, the question of suffering is a mystery and while theologians may write lengthy tomes and preach impassioned sermons, they do not really *know* the answer to the eternal questions.

It is, however, important that we be clear about one issue, and that is concerning anger with God. Because we are in awe of the majesty and power of God there is a natural tendency to feel that it is blasphemous to be angry with Him; perhaps at a hidden level, too, we are afraid that, like Job, we might get an answer that we are not big enough to handle or that some divine ray gun will reduce us to a charred remnant. A closer glance at the book of Job, however, should clarify the issues, for we find that not only does God prefer Job's fury to the mealy-mouthed obeisance of the Comforters*, but that he does in fact listen to his complaints, even if Gods answer is not quite what Job expects. There is, throughout the Old Testament, a long tradition of God's friends arguing with him. We see it in Moses as he protests his unsuitability for the mission imposed upon him, in Jacob as he wrestles with the angel and in the wretched Jeremiah as he complains that the Lord has been playing fast and loose with him:

---

* Job's Comforters: four pious men who tell Job that God is punishing him and that he must mind his language.

10

'You have seduced me, Lord, and I have let myself be seduced;
you have over powered me: you were the stronger.
I am daily a laughing stock,
everybodys butt.'   Jer. 20.7

'Job, like Jeremiah, curses the day of his birth:
May the day perish when I was born,
and the night that told of a boy conceived.'   Job 3.3

It is important to understand, when dealing with the afflicted that
desperate men and women will often cry out in despair 'Why did
God let this happen to me? I wish I were dead!' when what they
really mean is: 'It's not fair! I wish it would all go away. I can't
cope with what's happening to me. Please help me.' They are like
a bewildered, terrified child kicking and screaming in it's
mother's arms. In the same way that a child must cry, so too must
an adult express his pain and anger. We must beware of trying to
step in between the grieving person and God like an officious
nanny saying self righteously 'Now, now, big boys don't cry.
Mummy wouldn't like you to say things like that'. Instead, I
believe, we should gently push the sufferer right into the arms of
God, flailing fists, clenched teeth, snotty nose and all; the place
for a desperate child is his parents arms. It may well be, of course,
that the grieving feel estranged, alienated from God and can find
no comfort in prayer. All we can do then is 'hold' them, if they
will let us, and encourage them to vent their fury reminding them
that God is big enough to take their anger and will answer them
in his own time. The difficulty, of course, is that God's time is not
necessarily our time.

Coping with tragedy

After this digression let us return to our drama. The curtain rises
on Act Two, Scene One, and we are back in Joanna's house.
Some months have passed and Jo's wild grief has abated. We find
her talking to her pastor and listen in amazement to the way she
has coped with her tragedy. 'God has been very good to me,' she

11

says with a gentle smile. 'I've had a wonderful loving husband and ten beautiful children. If God has chosen to take them from me, then that's his business. I can only trust him and try to rebuild my life.' Father Michael is silent in the face of a faith which he feels is a great deal stronger than his own. How on earth has this woman come to terms with such a tragedy in less than a year? Anyone else would have been completely destroyed, lost their faith, gone mad. (This is not a treatise on bereavement so I will resist the opportunity to explore the issue of whether or not Jo has come to terms with her loss or is somehow suppressing her grief, and move on to the next part of our story.

In Act Two, Scene Two, we are back in the court of heaven, where God is once again deep in conversation with Satan. 'What did I tell you? says God. 'You all but destroyed that poor girl's life and look, her faith is even stronger. *Now* are you satisfied? Satan, of course is not satisfied, 'Ah', he says: 'She's only lost her family. It's not as if she's had to suffer in her own body. I'll bet you if I really had a go at her it would be a different story.' God scowls. Clearly he feels trapped. If he continues his embargo on Jo's person, Satan will always be able to say. 'You haven't *really* tested her: If you lay a finger on her bone and flesh, I'll warrant you, she will curse you to your face.'

Eventually, God gives in and Satan goes off at speed to find Jo before God can change his mind. (If you find your hackles rising at this irreverent description of God, please go at once and read the Job story in your Bible. Like the writer there, I am using this caricature for a very serious purpose.)

The curtain falls and rises again on Scene Three and of course, the worst has happened. Jo is in hospital, struck down by cancer. She is a pitiful sight, a bowed figure parked in a wheel chair in the Radiotherapy Department corridor. She has lost her hair as a result of chemotherapy and she clutches a vomit bowl desperately on her lap. The tears run unchecked down her pinched cheeks and like Job she mutters to herself:

12

'It's not fair. I'm so miserable.
I feel so awful. Just look at me,
bald as a coot with my bones all sticking out.
Why is God doing this to me?
He's poisoned my body, my soul,
everything I ever loved.
What ever have I done to deserve this.
How could God be so cruel?'

Poor Jo. What on earth can we say to her? Better perhaps to say nothing, and leave her in the hands of the kindly porter and the nurse who have mercifully appeared to take her back to the ward. My world is populated by the likes of Jo. Sometimes they get better and leave hospital to live happily ever after; more often, perhaps, they die, or linger on for months in indifferent health, asking the same terrible question: 'Why me? What have I done to deserve this? How can there be a loving God if he treats his children like this?'

While much of pastoral care is best done by listening, by sharing the afflicted person's darkness of rage and despair, there comes eventually, the time to speak, to try to explain the inexplicable, to make sense of tragedy. What then? What are we to say? There are, I believe, certain basic guidelines to help us in answering these 'why suffering' questions: the first is that we must speak only from our own knowledge and experience, from our own truth. We *all* feel inadequate in trying to answer these questions but if *we* have been asked, it is *our* ideas that are being sought, not those of the vicar down the road. This may mean that we sit there empty handed saying weakly: 'truly I don't understand what's going on, but I do believe that God is somehow here in the mess with you and that he loves you.' This may well be enough. If it isn't, and you don't know where to go from there, its best to suggest the person speak to someone with some theological expertise. The second guideline is that, as always, we must temper our answer to the condition of the questioner. It is no earthly use my quoting great tracts of Job, however much they

13

may help *me*, to someone to whom that kind of language is totally alien. Similarly, its not a lot of use telling those who are plunged into despair and unbelief that Jesus died to save them and everything will be alright in heaven. As a Christian I actually believe precisely that: but as a pastoral carer I know that this kind of language is frequently unhelpful to those whose faith is under strain.

An explanation

Let me assume, however, for our purposes that I am being questioned by someone who is *not* acutely grieving, who believes in God and in Christ but who is grappling, as we all do, carers and sufferers alike, with the problem of suffering. It is at this stage of our exploration that we should go together to the original text of Job and listen (for this is a very dramatic speech) to the opening words of God as he addresses the wretched, complaining, Job.

> 'Who is this obscuring my designs
> with their empty headed words?
> Brace yourself like a fighter;
> now it is my turn to ask questions
> and yours to inform me.
> Where were you when I laid the earth's foundations?
> Tell me, since you are so well informed!
> Who decided the dimensions of it, do you know?
> Or who stretched the measuring line across it?
> What supports its pillars at their bases?
> Who laid its corner stone
> When all the stars of the morning were singing for joy,
> and the Sons of God in chorus were chanting praise?
>
> On and on the questions come:
> Who pent up the sea behind closed doors
> When it leaped tumultuous out of the womb,
> When I wrapped it in a robe of mist
> and made black clouds its swaddling bands;

Have you ever in your life given orders to the morning
or sent the dawn to its post,

Have you journeyed all the way to the source of the sea,
or walked where the Abyss is deepest?
Have you been to the gates of Death
or met the janitors of Shadow land?'

(after) Job 38

There is not space here to quote as much of the Lord's answer to
Job as I would like, but it is wondrously powerful and beautiful
and I urge you to read it, for it is in these last chapters that the
answer to our questions lies hidden. I say 'hidden' because while
God's answer to Job is written in a style and idiom accessible to
the people of a particular culture living over two thousand years
ago it is less readily available to us. Let us return, therefore, to the
imagery of our own time, to where we began, with the lovely and
virtuous Joanna. We left her, you will recall, plunged once more
into darkness, this time with her own personal physical affliction.
Like Job, she wails in distress and then, having summoned up all
her strength, she demands an answer of God. 'What are you
playing at God?' she says. 'What have I done to deserve this?
Haven't I always served you to the best of my ability? You took
away my husband and my children, and I accepted it all as your
will. And now you are doing this to me? What's going on? I've a
right to know!'

And then, out of the whirlwind, perhaps in a dream, perhaps in
the darkness of her despair in that hospital corridor, the answer
comes – but its not what Jo expects, just as it was not what Job
expected:

'My little one, you just don't know what you are talking about.
The earth is infinitely more mysterious and complicated than
you can possibly understand:

Where were you when I made the human body, fashioned it,
bone and sinew, in its magnificent intricacy of form? Have you

15

any idea of the delicate balance of your immune system? What happens in your cells when a piece of genetic material changes and a rogue cell takes off like a terrorist, planting onco-genes throughout your body like fire bombs in a department store? Has it ever occurred to you that such a delicately balanced organism will by its very nature break down from time to time? Don't you realize that you are part of the earth? What would happen to the planet if you and your family lived forever, you would end up huddled together like discarded plastic containers on a deserted beach.'

I could go on and on like the author of Job, but it would be no more comprehensible. The message of Job, as I understand it, is this: God's creation is as it is. It is infinitely wild and complex and we cannot hope to understand it all. Creation is also closely interdependent. Our human life is part of an inter-locking system of nature and creatures, of a universe that is not static, but changing. It is of the very nature of our world that there is violence in it. The earth's crust is alive, it moves and volcanoes erupt. Animals prey upon each other: if they didn't the veldts and prairies would be full of old and sick and dying animals. People prey upon each other. Men and women are fragile, wounded creatures: they are insecure, suspicious, afraid of the unknown, afraid of losing what they have and they guard their space and their possessions jealously. Human beings are alive as the earth and its creatures are alive: they have sexual desires, passions, lusts which they sometimes cannot control. They rape, pillage, murder, for survival, for gain, for fun. That is the world in which we live, the world made by our all powerful creator God.

But it is also a world of incredible beauty, of mountains and sunsets, of glaciers and lush green valleys. It is the world of the seal, the dolphin and the polar bear, of the eagle, the humming bird and the territorial domestic robin. It is the world of poets and musicians, of ice skaters and ballet dancers, of scientists and geniuses of all kind. It is a world of heroes as well as of cowards, of saints as well as sinners, of dedicated men and women who

16

give their lives as a holocaust for those who cannot care for themselves. For every volcano erupting there are ten thousand quiet and fertile hillsides, for every rapist a hundred thousand lovers, whispering words of comfort, joy and ecstasy. This is the world that our God has made and, like the author of Genesis, I believe that it is very good.

So there you have your answer: 'Sorry Job, sorry Joanna, that's the way things are.' We can hardly say it's a very satisfactory answer, can we? And yet, it seems, Job *was* satisfied, for he says:

'I know that you are all powerful:
What you conceive, you can perform,
I am the man who obscured your designs
with my empty headed words,
I have been holding forth on matters I cannot understand,
on marvels beyond me and my knowledge.

*   *   *

I knew you then only by hearsay;
but now, having seen you with my own eyes,
I retract all that I have said,
and in dust and ashes I repent.'

Job 42. 2–6

The key to understanding Job's acceptance of God's answer lies in the penultimate two lines of this verse:

– 'I knew you then only by hearsay; but now I have seen you with my own eyes.'   Job

Beyond our understanding

Job can accept God's answer because it has come directly from God in a mind blowing personal encounter. Now that he has met God, Job realizes that his questions, although they seemed justified, were in fact irrelevant, *because his idea of God was all wrong.*

In the last chapters of the Book of Job, the carefully constructed stage set of the court of heaven with its God with a long white beard and Satan with his pitch fork are swept away. They disappear because they are only a fantasy, a projection, an invention of a people who have tried to fashion a God they can understand and control. The trouble is that we too are tempted to fashion idols, to project on to God all sorts of human qualities so that we can understand and therefore control him. But God is not like that. He is 'totally other'. He (She, It, They,) has existed from all time, is beyond our world, beyond our understanding. This is what we mean when we say that God is TRANSCENDENT, beyond all that we can understand.

This understanding of God is as old as man himself, as is the idea that God is like us. Men and women have always struggled to hold in tension the idea of the Divinity as utterly unknowable and mysterious and the idea of God as somehow accessible and concerned with our affairs. The primitive peoples resolved this tension by believing in a whole range of Gods, one of whom was unknowable and the others who were accessible. Before the revelation of Sinai, the Israelites aknowledged El Shaddai, the God of the mountain as the creator, the controller of mysterious events like fertility and the seasons, but they had their domestic Gods who travelled about with them, to whom they could tell their troubles and talk as a friend. The revelation at Sinai was a watershed event because if was the moment when God revealed that not only is he all powerful, transcendent and beyond all knowing, but he is also IMMANENT, that is close at hand, and that he loves his people with great passion. What God tries to teach his people in the first two commandments was that he was their only God and that they had no need of other Gods: they should approach him directly. He described himself to Moses: 'Yahweh, Yahweh, a God of tenderness and compassion, slow to anger, rich in kindness and faithfulness'. Exodus 34. 6

The Old testament is full of such descriptions of God. In the first chapter of Deuteronomy the Lord reminds his people of the time when he carried them 'as a man carries his child,' while in Hosea 11.3 we read:

'I was like someone who holds an infant
close against his cheek;
stooping down to him I gave him his food.'

Transcendent and Immanent

Again and again we hear this message: I, God, loved my people like a father, but they did not understand – they could not grasp the concept that a mysterious all powerful God was also good and loving. That is why the people of Israel made the golden calf: they just couldn't cope with the unseen God of Sinai; they had to have a God they could imagine and control. And we, of course are the same. We too find it hard to accept that God is as he is, and we make idols of him. Either he is a terrible dictator who doesn't care about us, or he is a loving daddy who would never hurt his children. When all goes well, we favour the second option, but when our world collapses, we say, like a frightened child, that daddy is wicked and cruel, and then we feel totally lost.

But there *is* another way. It *is* possible to integrate these two concepts of God, to learn that he is both transcendent and immanent, both beyond all knowing and as close to us as our mother's breast. It is the way of the scriptures, the way of the mystics and it is the way of Jesus, of Nazareth, Emmanuel, God with us. Perhaps God realized that is was just too hard for most people to cope with his 'otherness' and that is why he sent his Son so that we could see with our own eyes what God was like. But even in Jesus' own day it was hard, and Jesus was exasperated when one of the disciples asked:

'Lord, let us see the Father and then we shall be satisfied!'
'Philip!' Jesus said, 'Have I been with you all this time, and still

19

you do not know me . . . Do you not believe that I am in the
Father and Father is in me?'   John. 14. 8

Finally, let us try to integrate the Judaeo Christian understanding
of the mystery of suffering that is our spiritual heritage and
should be our support and our comfort. The message goes like
this: God, who is all powerful and infinitely mysterious made the
world. He made it in his own way, intricate and beautiful, wild
and dangerous. He filled it full of plants and living creatures, the
most complex and self aware of whom was man. God appointed
men and women as *stewards* of the earth, to live on it, to cherish
it but not to plunder and destroy it. It is in the nature of this
world, of all God's creatures, that they are frail and vulnerable
that they die. Nothing and no one lives forever. All matter is
eventually recycled, as people, as animals, as stardust. That is the
way things are. On this earth we are all sojourners, because we
are all destined ultimately to return to the Divine, to the heart of
God from whence we come.

If we were angels, of course, we would understand the truth that
death is not a tragedy, that it is quite simply the beginning of the
life for which we were originally created. But then we are not
angels, we are creatures and we see as Paul, puts it, 'through a
glass darkly'. How then can we not be sad when we or those we
love are afflicted or face death? This is what it means to be
human: to be frail and vulnerable in our bodies, to be storm
tossed in our emotions, to be limited in our understanding. We
forget, however that this is the way the One Holy Transcendent
God made people and that, when he had finished he smiled upon
his work and declared that it was very, very good.